Little things from here & there

AF527356

Achyut Joshi

BookLeaf Publishing

Presentation by *BookLeaf Publishing*

Web: www.bookleafpub.com

E-mail: info@bookleafpub.com

ISBN: 9789357446013

First edition 2023

*To anyone who has ever doubted themselves,
push through!*

The beginning

ना मूज़े हिन्दी आती है, and neither my English is perfect.
But I love writing और में लिख रहा हू |

में वो हू जो अपने आप में रहता है, But my shells collapse like dominos,
जब में लिख रहा होता हू , And I am writing.

Is it worth it?

Has anyone felt that sheer guilt from within?
something inside you wants to curse you,
break you, punch you and pull you down the stairs
into the infinite void till you cannot match your own sight

I have. And I have known this for long.
But still I did nothing.

Four long years back, I left home to pursue my dreams.
I was always taught to dream big and,
fortunately or unfortunately,
I dreamt bigger that my cosy little home city could provide.

There was this unsaid understanding that
one day I will leave home, but never really understood that
I will never really be at home after that day.

Family gatherings started to become a rarity,
Home-food a luxury and festival days just holidays.

But more importantly, I was never there
I was never there for them, when they needed
the most.

When they wanted to learn a new app,
When they were facing issues with their
mobiles,
When they wanted to be in sync with the modern
world
or when they just wanted a kid in the house.
They were always there, always.
They still are, and here I am,
trying to open my wings and fly away
when all they want is to fly with me.

Is it really worth it?
The success. The knowledge
The degrees. The work.
When you are not with the people
because of whom you are in this tangled world
the first place.

Is it really worth it?

The Walk

Wagging tail, a jump worthy of a zillion score,
and a bark loud as a roar.
Do you want to see happiness?
Come to my house at five!

I walk down the stairs,
with sleep smelling everywhere in the air.
And though I try not to make a din,
he picks it up on my first step in.

He knows. He jumps. And he barks.
It is his usual time for an evening stroll.

He walks me around,
taking me through humps of trash on the ground.
And only after the inspection of every stone,
and peeing in every corner on the road
does he return to his humble home.

Do you want to see happiness?
Come to my house at five!

That bastard is our family's pride.
Of all the happiness he has brought to this
house,

I would be the most indebted,
to my parent's second child
for being there when I was not.

Do you want to see happiness?
Come to my house at five!
Because my fierce four-legged brother
comes out for a walk!

Dark beauty

My first time with you was not how I had
expected.
Well, to be frank, I never knew you will become
a big part of me.

I still remember that night, a little too drunk
in the shivery silence of the Thar desert.
In my senses, I would not have agreed to the
ride,
but the rum worked its charm.
We were in the middle of nowhere,
with darkness blanketed all around us,
and that night I learnt
that you bare all only far from the city lights.
And, there I saw you in all your glory.
I laid back on the sand,
caring the least about my clothes or the cold.
Just gazed at the infinite void that was you.
You, The night sky!

Ever since that fateful night,
I yearn to chase you
in different places, and on different nights.
Right from the rocky desert in the Spiti,
to the breezy beaches of Thailand.
And not once you have failed to stun me.

The brilliance of the silence that comes
with your black maddening darkness.
The magnanimity that grows by beholding
the vastness of your existence.

Oh, my! Oh, my!
I pity those whose mere acquaintance with you
is amongst the city lights.

For they have not seen the black princess
freckled with diamonds on her side,
whose mere presence teaches you
about our infinitesimal extant.
And above all, you are hope.
You are the healing dark!

Tears

Have you ever knowingly gone into a rabbit hole of memories?
Like one youtube video, leads to another
And then you stare at that one picture on your hard disk!
Your mind is screaming to stop, but you don't.
You can't.
You want to. But you can't.

Living alone, away from home has been tough on me,
Most of the days, I have this mask on.
A mask that I am sure my old friends would never believe I could wear.
I am described as an extrovert, someone who can easily laugh on himself,
and someone who can easily talk to people.
This is exactly someone who I wanted to become a few months back.
And when I am almost there, why do I miss my old self?

On somedays, which recently have become quite common,
I finally let go off that mask, but only when I am alone.
And that too for a few minutes, and I breathe.
I let go, and I cry.

Tears, the most under rated medicine to sadness,
has unfortunately or fortunately
become my best friend these days.

Family recipe

Take out a big pan & wash it clean.
Bring the fresh veggies from your office bag
and soak them in water.
While you wait, open youtube and search
"Easy ways to make paneer bhurji"

As you scroll through,
you realise how bad you are at cooking.
Living alone for the first time was tough indeed.
But it felt bad when you had to cook alone.

You give up and FaceTime the only person in
this world,
who can make even the ugliest looking food,
yummy - Mom.

Now, every mom is a Da vinci is her own right.
She orders to show the ingredients at your
disposal.
She pauses for a minute, maybe thinking
of what can be made out of this mayhem.

"Heat up the pan, and put some oil.
Cut the onions and tomatoes
and let them fry"- she starts!

And suddenly dad comes on the call
and like always he starts telling his recipe -
Add 2 pinches of Pav Bhaji Masala
and let the onions turn brown he says!

After thirty minutes, you have something
that resembles the curry you intended to make.
Though you are not sure who's recipe it is -
your mom's or your dad's!

You change to your front camera,
so your folks can admire their creation.
In that moment, you realize that it is everyone's
recipe!
Your mom's technique, your dad's spices
and of course your execution!

You quickly end the call
so you can finally eat the food.
Although the salt was off, and it was a bit too
spicy
that was the best paneer bhurji you will ever
have
and you exactly know why!

Words

Words have always been my closest friend,
A friend that you call up at 2am,
When you are shivering with anxious thoughts.
And just by their presence, you feel good.

I, me, myself.

I, me, myself.
Some call them selfish,
Some call them self-obsessed.
But i call them the North Star.

Guilty as charged,
I was one of those some.
Searched for meaning
In things and faces around.

And I got lost,
Deep into an abyss, alone.
Don't get me wrong,
there were voices to guide.
But it was I, me, and myself
Who had to climb out.

I say this,
Don't let the 'I' get lost,
Because at the end,
that is your North Star,
The tiny light
at the end of a tunnel.

And if you find yourself,
In the abyss like me.
Just trust the I,
They gotchu.

I, me, myself.
Some call them selfish,
Some call them self-obsessed.
But I call them the North Star.

Bruno

I lost a brother last year,
And I was 20 time zones away.

the memory of my last visit is fresh,
the last touch still in flesh
he was ailing, and in excruciating pain.
And yet trying hard to remain.

The day he died, I had a hunch
that the end was coming as such.

On my usual evening run,
I got a call from my dad, he said, "son!"
With the heaviest sigh and the loudest cry
"Bid your brother a goodbye"

The world stood still, and I couldn't believe.
That out of thin air, he could just leave.
I always wonder, what he felt
In his last minutes before he left.

Maybe I know, maybe I don't know.
But I know that his name was Bruno,
He was my fierce four legged brother,
And I try to find him in every dog I discover

Master of my own fate

A gush of hot air swept passed me,
As I walked into the JFK international airport.

I was making a sudden trip to India,
It was less of a vacation,
more of a cry for help.

Gazes were set on me
As I made my way through the airport,
sneezing like a mad man.

While standing in the long queue,
The last few months went past me.
My startup was failing,
I was going through a divorce
And yet, I had not shed tears.
I was at my lowest, in the darkest of places.

Right in the middle of those thoughts,
Someone knocked my luggage over,
They apologized, I smiled knowing that
they don't know how
close I am to giving up.

I remembered Vir Das's words, he says,
Buy an expensive dinner on your bad days,
While eat the cheapest meal on your good.

The next moment,
I find myself sitting in first class,
Having paid more than double the price.
But here I was flying first class
For the first time, when I was about to give up.

To that I toast,
Life! I will always own the moment, and
I am indeed the master of my own fate.

The dreamers

The millennials, the dreamers, the travelers,
The generation who eat breathe and live
technology.
We have been called by a lot of names,
Cursed for living in the moment,
Insulted for being the orthodox-breaker.
But you know what I love the most about us -
We fuckers do what we want to.

Breathing again

With shattered dreams, I fell down,
Life's storms had left me to drown,
But with each breath, I rose anew,
Stronger, wiser, and with a clearer view.

Mirror

The reflection staring back at me,
Was once a stranger I couldn't see,
But with each day and every choice,
I learned to love and hear my own voice.

Best days of my life

The day came. It started.
And it was the toughest day of my life.
10th May it was.
The day when we parted,
the day when I changed.

We had stayed up all night
Four of us were leaving by a morning train.
A planned sober night, which turned into
a night of a couple of whiskey shots.
And for the final time,
and maybe the last,
we were all together in one room.

Promises of meeting again,
tight hugs to show our love,
and moist eyes.
And as the clocks neared 5 am,
we took a final walk of our home,
laid down on the misty grass
and watched the stars in silence
a silence filled with a million of
conversations and emotions.

Railway stations and airports
are a mecca of goodbyes and farewells.
I finally gave up and let the tears flow
The final hug, the final glance
and the green signal
We were four down!

It should never have been this tough.
But then if we had the guts
to build a friendship this strong,
Tears ought to come.

Finally, in the evening my time was up.
We had somehow gotten used to saying
goodbyes.
So with simple hugs and
a wide smile on my face,
I boarded the same train,
on which I had started this journey.

So dear me,
This is how it ended.
A big part of us died that day,
a part that will be remembered,
cherished and missed for the days to come.

Life completes a full circle.
I cried on the first day,
because I was scared of what lied ahead.

And I cried on the last day,
because I was leaving a part of me behind.

We will meet on the road

We'll meet on the road

She sits there alone on the best table in the eatery,
a book, a notepad, a pack of cigarettes
& a little purse rests on the wood.
There is no gown or a stomper to impress,
just rugged jeans with a solid tee
and the hair made into a bun.
A perfect sight showcasing
all the struggles of being on road
and yet radiates an eternal sense of calm.

Thats my girl. And we'll meet on the road.

Millennials are known to be obsessed with traveling.
the excitement of discovering
the secrets behind every crossing,
the sheer joy of waking up daily to new somethings,
and the nirvana of having a place grow on you.

But seldom do we realize
the perils of being on the road.

you sometimes lose yourself
in the process of finding the real you.

So, there she is,
engrossed in her book
as the sun sets over the horizon.
As I sit down, I accidentally knock of a spoon
and she nonchalantly fixes her gaze on me.

Thats my girl. And we'll meet on the road.

Colours

With every sunrise, you start the morning afresh.
A clean slate, with an infinite colors to choose.
Doesn't matter if the night was good or bad.
Just paint, and see the magic unfold

Little things from home

घर, Home
A place where the first thing we say when we enter is "जय श्री कृष्णा".
I wouldn't consider myself a believer in god and yet,
I have always entered my house saying those words.
It just felt correct, felt like home!

A place where we always find an ever enthusiastic creature,
waiting for us quietly at the door.
Bruno, our dog, a fierce little brother,
jumps and wags his tail every time
we open that big old green gate
as if he is seeing us after months!

A place where everything has a habit, a tradition.
Like lunches, All the three of us,
sitting at the dining table,
dad on the left, I on the right
and my mom in the centre.
Or, mom dad kissing me goodbye
every time I went to school,

even in the 12th grade.
Embarrassing at that time,
but I do miss it today when I walk out alone
everyday.

A place where I follow a strange ritual every
time I leave.
Before rushing out of my room,
I walk around, roll my hands on furniture
and I stand in the middle,
close my eyes and say, “I will be back soon”.
And slowly as dad drives us
either to the airport or the train station,
I take a last glimpse of this magnificent home ,
and ask her to protect them.

So you know, home is not just a feeling.
It is the very thing that protects this beautiful
tiny world.
A world that my parents have worked so hard to
create.

Until we meet again

I am not amongst the most talkative people.
I have a shell around me that cracks open
only when I write. And I am writing!

And I love living,
और मैं जी रहा हूँ।

www.ingramcontent.com/pod-product-compliance
Ingram Content Group UK Ltd.
Pitfield, Milton Keynes, MK11 3LW, UK
UKHW021414280325
5209UKWH00034B/657

9 789357 446013